CENTRES for the SERVANTS

Parish Plant up-dated

KENNETH WHITE

GROVE BOOKS   BRAMCOTE   NOTTS.

CONTENTS

OUR CHURCH doesn't work any longer is a prevailing complaint of clergy, P.C.C.s and those members of the congregation who are trying to relate the language of the liturgy to the talk of the laundrette.

Of course, they mean the church *buildings* and in most cases they are right. We no longer sit on wooden benches at home, so why endure pews in church? The New Series forms of worship integrate parson and people, as the Book of Common Prayer does, yet church plant divides them.

This booklet is the sequel to SHRINES FOR THE SAINTS, which ought preferably to be read first and which outlines the way Christians have enclosed their peculiar activities from the early Church to the present day. We now turn to to-morrow and the next day and ask *In the light of tradition and an analysis of today's (and tomorrow's) needs, what ought we to do about our church buildings?*

A fair question?

Cover Picture: St. Francis' Church
Duston, Northampton

Copyright Kenneth White, 1975

First Impression December 1975

ISSN 0306 0608

ISBN 0 901710 80 6

CENTRES FOR THE SERVANTS

Our possessions will have to go, including many of those buildings of small historic value which do little more than consume our money and our energies.
The truth is that when confidence revives, and love of God waxes warm, and faith burns bright, financial problems have a strange way of solving themselves.

Donald Coggan, Archbishop of Canterbury,
in his enthronement sermon, 24 January 1975;
the reign of Queen Elizabeth II.

A Christian engaged in market-place evangelism invited a stranger to a church Guest Service. 'No thanks', replied the stranger, 'I've got enough troubles already'.

So has the Church; it always had. From the Colosseum to Coventry there has been change and controversy. Most of the time the Church's life-style has been reflected in its buildings. We have now reached the situation when (let's face it) many of our church premises (including halls) are a handicap.

Propagating the Gospel is difficult enough without the frustration of buildings which hamstring our progress. Holy stones have become millstones.

Not everywhere, of course. Some of our church buildings are superb architecture, works of art in their own right. This excellence transcends period, applying to Victorian as well as Norman, though the rediscovered notion of conservation is often uncritical and sentimental.

A driver meeting an unknown parson at London Airport approached a likely-looking man and enquired whether he was a clergyman. 'No', replied the stranger, 'I'm just having a nasty bout of indigestion.'

Unkind to parsons? Of course; but how much indigestion is caused by church premises which no longer function adequately? More important, how much *spiritual* indigestion?

In spite of redundancy, most of our churches must soldier on. They will need regular building maintenance and continuing upkeep; and they are not usually the most economical piles to be repaired—or heated!

So what to do?

1 OVER OUR SHOULDER

Before we can make proposals we must take stock of our church.

> *Historically* . . . where does it fit chronologically?
> *Functionally* . . . how do we use it?
> *Capacity* . . . how big is it?

Historically This is the contents of SHRINES FOR THE SAINTS, the companion booklet; but a precis is worthwhile here as a reminder.

The planning of Christian worship houses has evolved down the centuries. Sometimes worship has set the pace; at other times building has led the way. Always architecture and worship have reacted reciprocally, though in any given period of the Church's development the building has come to subserve the activity within it.

In the early Church, believers were more truly grouped in 'households of God', families of Christians, These were based on domestic premises, usually of generous size.

Growth in numbers led to the basilica church, with an organised congregation. J. P. Audet's truism 'Numbers necessarily change the form and content of human relations' operated when family instruction expanded into public preaching. The danger of large congregations is always the loss of closely-knit household fellowship; certainly by medieval times the ordained Christians had withdrawn themselves into a separate worshipping class. In consequence, multi-compartment, closely-screened churches reflected this withdrawal ethos. Chancels and chapels accommodated the clergy, nave and side aisles the people; up to the mid-16c.

After the 1550s the same buildings were adapted to Prayer Book liturgy. This brought clergy and people together as a worshipping partnership, leaving the chancel as a Communion room.

In the 17c a new church shape was devised, harking back to the old basilica layout and with emphasis on audibility. This was closely matched by non-Conformist meeting-houses.

These new auditory churches and (to varying extents) the re-arranged medieval churches suited the Prayer Book, which is mainly a *spoken* rather than a *visual* liturgy—and is fully congregational. Orientation was no problem and box

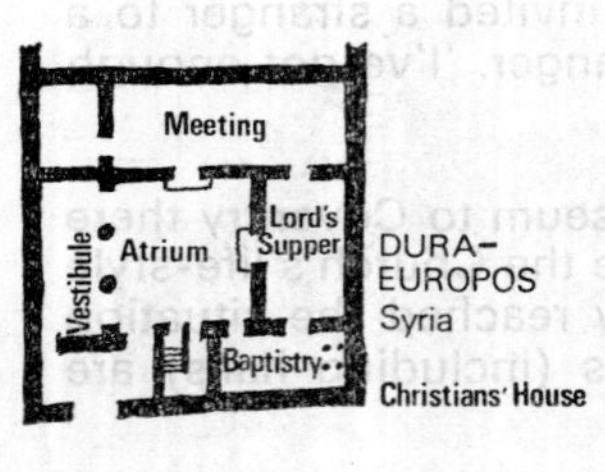

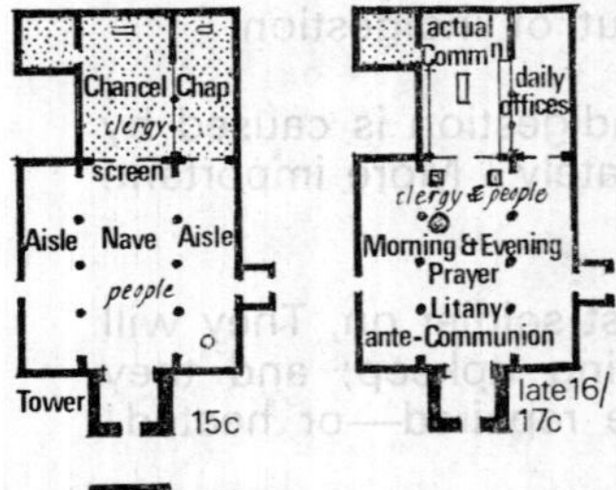

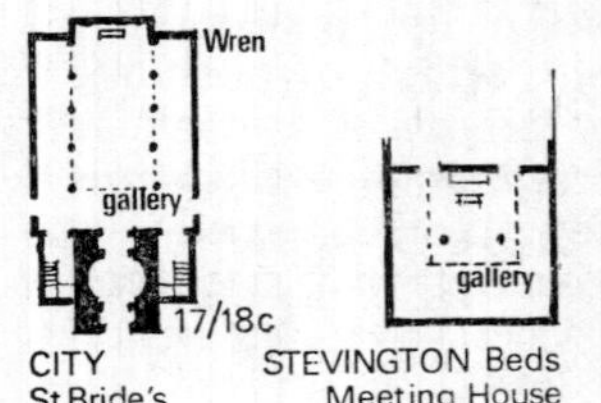

pews were widespread. A classical style of architecture was normal with notional Gothic appearing here and there.

With the Victorian harkback to pre-Reformation attitudes, the Church of England reverted to Gothic styles of architecture and ritualistic practices; Gothic Revival forms also afflicted non-Conformist premises.

It began with the Tractarian (or Oxford) Movement in the 1830s, led by Keble, Pusey, Newman and others who longed to see the Established church revitalized. Lethargy and abuse had pervaded the life of the Church and the effects of the Evangelical revival under Wesley were waning. 'This was the state of affairs (says a publication by the Essex Record Office) that the leaders of the Oxford Movement set out to remedy. In spite of all the controversy they aroused, they did succeed in transforming the worship of the Church of England. Their aim was to restore to the rather drab and perfunctory usages of the Church the mystery and ceremonial that had vanished at the Reformation. This included more frequent celebration of the Communion and more attention to the liturgical side of services. The Movement influenced not only the pattern of worship but the whole style of ecclesiastical architecture. It was particularly successful in industrial parishes where the churches provided an element of colour which was lacking in everyday life and where the clergy often wore themselves out in the service of the poor'.

It is questionable whether the transformation would have been so complete if the initiative had remained at Oxford. The campaign was enthusiastically adopted by a group of undergraduates at Cambridge who founded the Cambridge Camden Society in 1839. They pursued the study of 'ecclesiology', the relationship between architecture and forms of worship. They prosecuted a crusade for a narrowly-defined style of architecture, for furniture layout contrary to previous centuries and for ritualism undreamt of for 300 years. Many of our familiar ceremonies and church arrangements derive from the mid-19c and sprang from Camden Society promulgations. There are very few churches today which retain their pre-Tractarian arrangements *in toto.*

The Victorians doubled our stock of churches, staffed them with sartorially elegant clergy and added more than a touch of theatre to their performance. It could be said that they rewrote the liturgical scenario in a spirit of pseudo-medieval pietism and unbrookable confidence.

The eventual reaction was a loss of nerve and the first 50 years of this century produced almost no progressive architectural or liturgical format; the last 25 years have shown positive trends in both. These dispositions are still maturing and apply architecturally to new premises as well as old ones remodelled; both are accommodating contemporary expressions of Christian vigour, eloquence and appeal. We are beginning to experience what Edwin C. Lynn terms 'full-functioning environment' in our church premises.

2 THE LEGACY

Following this brief historical background we can now investigate our heritage and consider present-day *usage* of our church premises. Obviously the *size* of the building and the congregation will affect this.

Because town and country churches come in such a range of shape, style and furnishing, and because there is such a marked lack of uniformity in ceremonial, we can only deal generally.

We start where it hurts: with our pocket.

The maintenance of any building is now costly and is proportional to its size. Churches are among the most expensive buildings to maintain—and funds are hard to come by. They are lofty (not least Victorian ones), draughty and uninsulated; heating costs are therefore relatively high. There is too much elbow room, de-scaling the worshipper in contrast. But the major drawback is the internal arrangement; rigid furniture (and too much of it) often uncomfortable, spread from one end to the other—and that can be quite a distance!

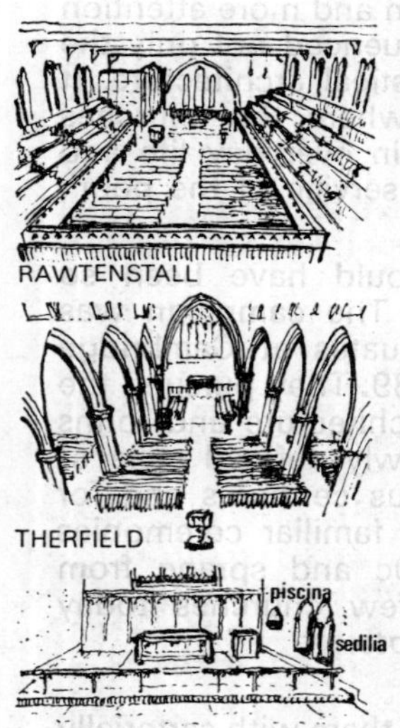

Let's pause and look at this layout. Most of our churches have a Victorian set-up: straight, hard pews; lectern balancing the pulpit; clergy stalls lifted up, probably behind a wall or screen, and with choir stalls stretching away, swallowing up the (shrinking) robed choir, the whole ensemble focussing on a display at the east end with the holy table in various states of dress or undress. Behind the table there may be a reredos and in front, the rails. On the right of it a credence table and various recesses in the walls: piscina (or basin), sedilia (or seats).

This is by no means all the equipment. At the opposite end there is the font, possibly a gallery and host of cupboards, shelves and bric-a-brac. A Litany desk may obstruct the centre gangway and the organ will doubtless interpose somewhere.

Such is the range of furniture for worship, from which the ministers lead the proceedings and the people join in. This includes not only Sunday services but also weddings, funerals and other so-called Occasionals. Periodically there may be choral works, drama or other presentations.

These are some of the activities for which the building must cater. We may well ask whether some of this furniture is functional—or even superfluous! Moreover, many a church is more like a mausoleum than a place for the living. Apparatus and vestures unheard of before 1840 are commonplace today. Forms of worship are diverse and often in antique language. In short, most of us in the Church of England worship under Victorian procedures rather than the post-Reformation economy which better interpreted the spirit of the Prayer Book—and would also suit the New Series today. Our present paraphernalia inculcates the impression that institutional Christianity is irrelevant and only for those with outmoded notions.

However, despite these handicaps, faithful congregations meet in much-loved and cared-for buildings, for which there is claimed a sense of God's presence and an atmosphere of *reverence.* This may be true and valid . . . but is often overstated. It then gives rise to the term 'House of God'. This is presumptuous and limiting; it is also an Old Testament term and has no place in the Gospel: 'the Most High does not live in houses made by men' (Acts 7.48). Even Solomon subscribed to this truth (2 Chronicles 6.18). Moreover, the coming of Christ's Spirit has shattered the concept of a localised deity; yet we still hear of children peeping behind the frontal to see if God is at home! NOT the House of God, please! but the **House of the Church.**

So much for tradition and its legacy. We move forward to consider what the House of the Church needs to make it an environment for effective Christian activity; in other words, its updated *use.*

3 THE USE AND THE USERS

'Christian activity'! What is this? Surely, to a Christian all his activity is Christian activity? This study must be limited to church activities, the assembling of the body of Christ.

> *Come to him, to that living stone, rejected by men but in God's sight chosen and precious; and like living stones be yourselves built into a spiritual house, to be a holy priesthood, to offer spiritual sacrifices acceptable to God through Jesus Christ.*
>
> 1 Peter 2.4, 5

Coming to him . . . to be built into . . . to be holy . . . to offer worship acceptable to God . . . however formal or diverse the ceremony might eventually become within the various churches. Our basic problem is therefore the enclosure of space for the activity of a special community within society.

> *You are a chosen race, a royal priesthood, a holy nation, God's own people, that you may declare the wonderful deeds of him who called you out of darkness into his marvellous light.*
>
> 1 Peter 2.9

If *worship* and *declaration* are therefore primary activities, there are many secondary church activities. Not all of these need be on-site. We may have off-site activities such as open-airs, home meetings, door-to-door and hospital visiting, and other goings-out. We must limit our study to on-site, mission station, branch office activities.

Consider straightforward worship services, mostly on Sundays and in the church. It matters little for this study whether these services are Series Infinity, pop Cranmer or curate's brainchild, whether a wedding or a parade service. Certain constants can be assumed:

There will be a leader, or leaders
All present will need to participate
There will be movement *(standing, kneeling, sitting, processing, acting maybe)*
Sound will be made *(speaking, singing, music)*

It is also desirable for everyone to prepare beforehand (even only a few moments' prayer) and to engage in Christian fellowship afterwards, lubricated by a welcome cup of coffee.

Bearing this in mind, what basic furniture is needed?

4 UTILITIES FOR THE USERS

Give the Leader a table. From it he could read any form of service and administer Holy Communion. He could place a portable font on it; he could preach from it. He need be no more elevated than is necessary for clear sight lines and hearing. For nearly 150 years churchmen have assumed that a sacramental table must dominate arrangements for public worship. Reference to Scripture may suggest that this constitutes over-emphasis; or wrong emphasis. For example, in Acts 2.42 the breaking of bread is not listed as the first activity to which the disciples devoted themselves.

The Participants, the congregation, require seating, maybe with kneelers and bookrests. If they are to come forward to receive the bread and wine at the Lord's Supper, they may need provision for kneeling as they gather round; the infirm certainly welcome a rail though there is a trend towards standing at the reception. The other participants will be the choir; choirs are diminishing in numbers, yet a trained group of vocalists can significantly encourage the congregational response. Their location is therefore important, either at the front (where they can be seen to give a lead) or at the rear (to back up the rest of the congregation). The choice is a local one and ought to promote corporateness in worship rather than conspicuousness in witness! As they

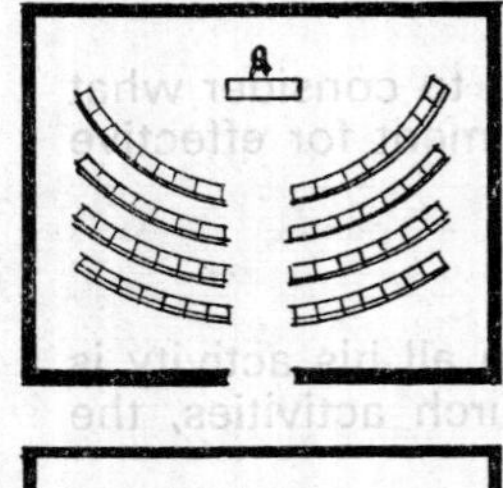

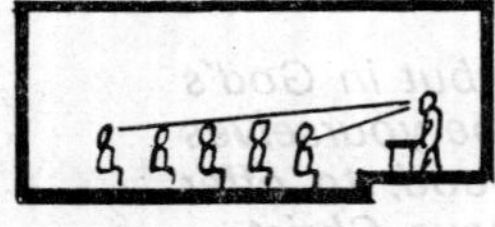

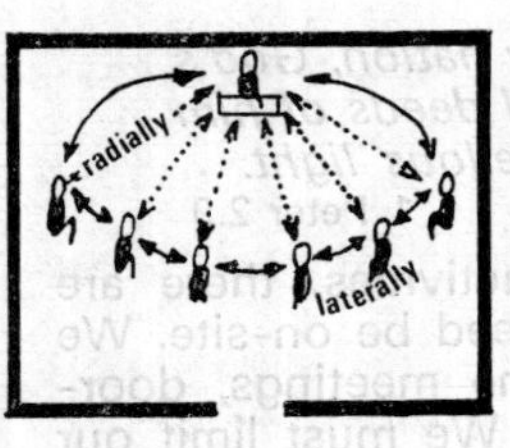

are unlikely to sing antiphonally, there is no need to adopt the Victorian symmetrical arrangement of angelic confrontation.

Music need not necessarily come from an organ and at certain services there may be other instrumentalists, on piano, guitar or harpsichord; a trumpet sounds exciting in a church with good reverberation. And there may be actors. These performers probably need no more than the dais on which the minister stands, with the portable table. Even so, they must be well positioned because music enriches worship and introduces a wider aesthetic than normal speech; against this must be admitted that most hymns are rarely well sung and the words are often turgid and incomprehensible. Perhaps we need conductors and verse-writers.

Audio-visual aids will need catering for, as well as utilitarian items such as bookstall and storage.

If all the furniture (except perhaps the organ) is portable, considerable flexibility will ensue. Orientation will present no problems and gangways can be set out as required. Civic services, weddings and special occasions may need a little formality.

The basics are therefore: a table (and chair), congregational (including choir) seating, dais, sundry accessories. To these we may add: reading desk(s), lectern, pulpit, fixed font, sundry tables, cupboards, hymnboards, flower stands . . . The danger is *clutter,* impairing the emphasis on people. We assemble in fellowship, to be the visible body of Christ; anything which detracts from our corporateness is therefore superfluous. This corporateness feeds on communication; and communication is basically relationships— between individuals and between groups. In church it will operate radially between minister and people reciprocally as well as laterally between everyone. When Christians come together, it is surely more than a time of mere withdrawal from the world? Communication involves proximity: visibility and audibility: sight lines and sound waves. Our furniture and its arrangement must support the proposition that Common Prayer is more than the sum total of individual devotions.

5 THE ENVELOPE

So much for the essential equipment to perform church services. What now of the architectural envelope? Obviously it must adequately enclose the range of activities within, but can the design influence spiritual vitality? The answer is that surely architecture must satisfy not only our *needs* but also our *aspirations.*

In new churches the site will bear an influence. The range of activities to be accommodated will affect the *size* of the building. So will the budget.

Externally, the building need not be monumental. It should certainly present a standing invitation to enter, appealing to the unbeliever as well as the Christian. The scale should be human (no longer are churches the highest buildings in the town) and there should be indications of relevance to life and death; this involves more than planting a cross on the front elevation.

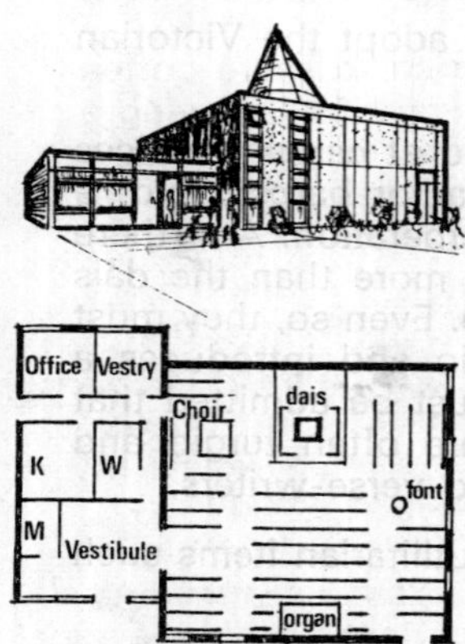

DUSTON St Francis

One example will suffice: St. Francis, Duston, Northampton. This is an economical structure using more factory-made components than normal traditional buildings. Of course, all buildings use industrial products and these have to be assembled on site, using a variety of wet and dry processes and a range of trades and equipment. At Duston, the components manufactured off-site are larger (*eg* concrete wall panels) than usual (*eg* bricks). Sited on a corner in a relatively new housing area, with a green opposite, this modest building is in the tradition of 18c meeting-houses. The simple glazed spire gives a strong hint of the function of the building and provides the interior with light and a sense of spaciousness. There are enough windows to rebuff any charge of Maginot retrenchment and they are nicely glazed. Furniture is simple, portable and limited. The congregation is gathered round so there is good communication, each person consciously part of the worshipping body; more so than when regimented into rows of pews.

The worship container will vary with local requirements, every solution being tailor-made, possibly following a full-scale social survey. It will be relatively straightforward when designing new premises, but what about older buildings, often gaunt, unlovely—and leaking?

6 OLD BOTTLES

Up and down England there is a vague dissatisfaction with the arrangements in parish churches. Usually it is inarticulate, but occasionally strong words are heard and determined action ensues. But there are often strong words *against* action and most schemes end in compromise. The risk lies in *tampering,* and ending up with modest adjustments which compound the irritation and please nobody. For example: the holy table at the far end of the chancel is often so remote that the vicar wonders if he is leading public worship or shouting the odds. So the table is brought forward, either to the chancel steps or even into the nave. Or a portable table is introduced; and portable rails. When these are used the choir is in limbo. If the choir stalls are removed, what happens to the chancel? And if space is tight at the front of the nave, how many pews do you remove?

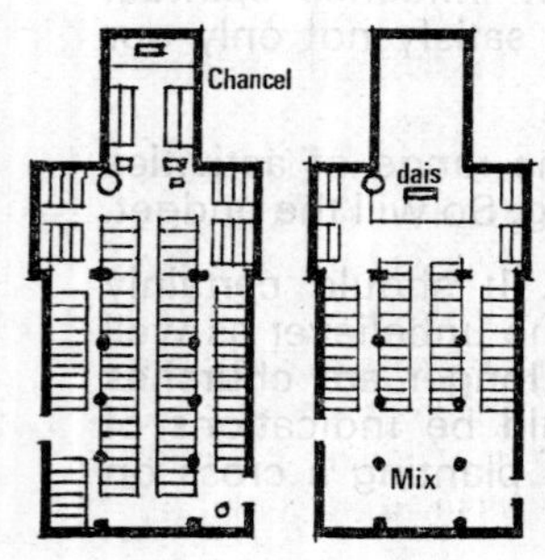

The same applies at the back of the church. If you wish to serve coffee after a service, what space do you require? And if it involves removing a couple of rows of pews, what about that raised plinth on which so many Victorian pews stand? Then there are those heating pipes . . . and the font . . . and hymnbook storage.

Height is another problem. Not all churches are majestic, so sometimes a suspended ceiling will improve acoustics and reduce heating costs.

Overriding these domestic debates are the Archdeacon, the Diocesan Advisory Committee and the Faculty procedure. Specialists on organs, wall paintings, brasses or stained glass (or even bells) may be called in; by this time the Incumbent and the Wardens are beginning to wonder . . .

It appears that the internal re-ordering of churches is not such a straightforward matter as we thought; no place, in fact, for ecclesiastical innocents. Alterations certainly require judgements based on knowledge, policy and open-mindedness; but most of all, based on prayer. It would be fair to expect that prayer is the commodity in plentiful supply when any exercise involving the church life is under consideration. Sadly, experience does not support this expectation. A true attitude of prayer supposes an openness to guidance and a seeking after the *right* solution. Instead, we find prejudice and preconception. Even more unfortunate is the situation where entrenched positions are adopted which are based on Victorian fallacies. Evangelicals often stand foursquare on usages which would have horrified their spiritual antecedents of 300 years back. Anglo-Catholics stoutly defend practices which the High Church Tories of pre-Victorian times would have considered sheer popery. Firm views are highly desirable after informed cogitation but 'I like what I like because I like it' is no basis for church policy. Let the knives be sheathed from start to finish.

7 SUNDAY IS NOT ALL CHURCH

We have pursued a modest research into basic furniture for Sunday worship in the church. We have discovered complications when trying to arrange existing plant.

Come back to our starting point in **4** (p.8): a table. A common move is to provide a holy table nearer the congregation. But if the east end table remains, what use is it? To let the chancel become a chapel may be no more than a stop-gap. We now have a different situation from the 17c and 18c when Communions were less frequent and the chancel was the Communion room. Nowadays a weekly parish or family Communion precludes that; but ought there to be more than one eucharistic centre in a church?

Statutory services are by no means the only parochial activity on Sundays. Sunday schools, Bible groups, youth fellowships abound; so do the titles and the age ranges. A great deal of solid teaching is undertaken on site. But where? Usually in that other parish structure.

There is nothing quite like an English church hall! An old one (20 years or more) is likely to have a characteristic bleak, unwelcoming atmosphere (outside and in) utterly removed from standards in our own homes. It is into these barns that we expect young people to assemble with joy and gladness!

Few churches have Sunday School in the afternoon so the peak period is Sunday morning. It is not uncommon to find vestries, cloakrooms, vicarage lounges (or even studies) pressed into service for this couple of hours once a week. Therefore, when considering building, there is a grave risk of designing for this peak period, only to discover later that realistic costing by the Quantity Surveyor rules out such a full course. No department store builds for the January sales.

Some have found the answer in a two-session system: 9.30 and 11; others, a blend of Family Service with half-time exodus of children to their groups, leaving the adults to hear a mature sermon. But leading a flock of small children a hundred yards down the road to the Hall (in the rain) is a depressing experience.

There is no standard solution and the local debate can be more than a little agonising. Yet it must be tackled. Building work is too expensive to be contemplated without responsible decision-taking.

Sunday evening services with follow-on meetings usually present less of an accommodation problem. There is, however, a trend which cuts across all we have said and which may complicate matters: coffee served to the congregation at the end of services. It is here that a peculiarly English phenomenon manifests itself. The congregation is apparently delighted to linger and sip coffee/tea and chat/gossip on the way out. Visitors are happy to be interviewed/quizzed. *So* welcoming; *such* fellowship! We *must* do this monthly/weekly!

But . . . if the congregation/visitors are obliged to go past an external door . . . don't bother to brew. Whooosh! at least half your customers will vanish. This will increase to 90% if you ask them to go out of the church and back into the hall.

8 MONDAY TO SATURDAY

We speak of certain church members being on 'full-time service', as if it were possible to be a part-time Christian! How strange then, that so many churches (the building) should be on part-time service! So part-time as to be deserted six days out of seven; and on the seventh to be in operation only three hours. What of the concept of full-time Christians in a full-time church? What kind of stewardship keeps an expensive building disused 95% of the week? What kind of businessmen are we? Surely this is gross extravagance?

Which brings us to Monday, Tuesday . . . At this point church activities become so diverse that even generalisations are not general enough. But we can try.

Basically, there are three categories of church activity, graded according to numbers:

1 The small group, up to 15 people, of any age. This will include Sunday School classes, Bible study groups, committees. Refreshments may not be required.
2 The medium-size meeting, up to 50 people. This takes in PCCs, youth clubs, women's meetings; including tea and biscuits.
3 The whole-church get-together for the Annual Meeting, a concert, supper, exhibition, bazaar, with full-scale catering. There may also

be such extra-parochial functions as deanery synods.

It is a useful exercise to prepare a schedule of every happening (including Sunday services, weddings, funerals) in the life of a local church during a 12-month period. Against each occasion, note the number attending and the facilities (catering, music, filmscreen) deployed. It might even be instructive to compare the size of the electoral roll at the beginning and end of the period!

It is a fair assumption that there are further activities which the vicar/curate/youth leader would like to initiate but which are inhibited by the premises available. Or a new slant given to present activities.

Why not prepare a second schedule setting out the pattern of church life *as it ought to be?*

Schedules, like graphs, are difficult to interpret; the situations they summarize are difficult to visualize. That is why television weather forecasts are pictorial. So sketch out a large diagram of church, hall and any other regularly available premises. These last might include the church day school, also no doubt under-used. But we'll return to this. The vicarage need not be included under 'available for parochial use'.

Allocate the activities already scheduled by writing them on the drawings of the various premises. You could even do this twice: first by locating the 12-month period meetings and services on the areas in which they actually occurred and, second, by allocating them where they ought to be located. At this point, the need for new or changed accommodation may begin to emerge. It is certain you will learn a great deal about the working (or non-working) of your church arrangements. By now the time has come to take the exercise a stage further.

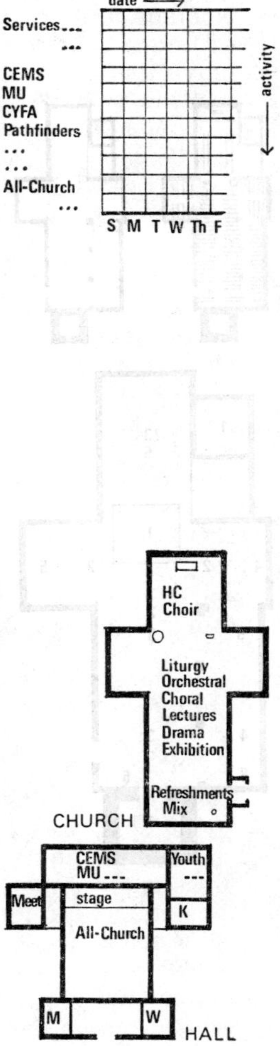

9 ROOT AND BRANCH

This booklet is dealing not only with new buildings but also the more common problem of re-ordering existing premises, with a special eye on concentrating activities into flexible space capable of intensive, and therefore economical, use. We may end up with less building and, in consequence, less maintenance costs. . . . .

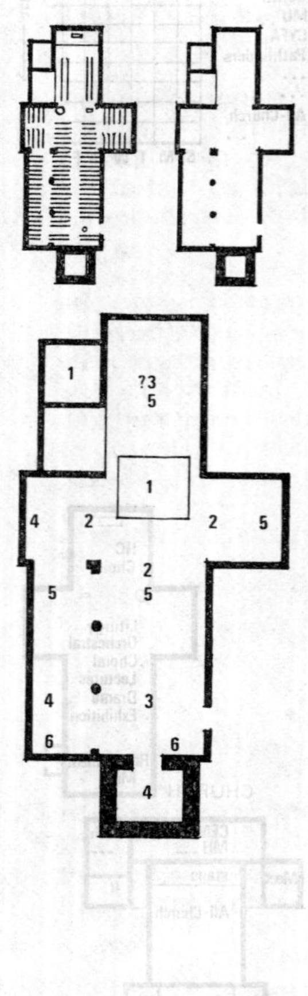

The procedure of the previous section was (1) to prepare schedules of activity and (2) convert these to geographical locations on rough plans of the available premises. We now come to (3) reconciling activities to accommodation. This is do-it-yourself planning.

Take the diagrams of your premises; mentally and with an indiarubber, remove all furniture. You now have the structure: floors, walls, roof, openings. You may also have substantial installations such as heating, organ and lavatories. There may be screens and historic artefacts; if they cannot be removed, plot them on the drawings. On these outline plans begin to doodle, preferably with a little discipline:

1 Locate on the church plan the working area(s) for Sunday services. We have seen that a dais with minimum furniture is called for.

2 Arrange seating with a close relationship to the working area; resist placing anyone behind the minister.

3 Allocate spaces for after-church milling about, or refreshments, or a meeting. This may be a Lounge, a Fellowship Area, a Foyer or a Parlour.

4 Consider spaces for other Sunday activities and their relationship to the foregoing.

5 Acknowledge weekday activities, trying as far as possible to gain multi-use of the above accommodation.

6 Add service areas: lavatories, cloaks, catering, storage, bookstall.

By now, the permutations are beyond a simple booklet; local conditions vary so widely.

The time has come to spread the load.

10 THE VOICE OF THE CONSTITUENCY

Laying hands on church people is fine, but laying hands on church buildings is quite another matter. The electoral roll will bristle. Yet here we are, with a suggestion that all is not well and we ought to do something . . . Maybe it is to suit the new vicar/curate with his modern ideas ('he actually addressed God as "You"; it'll be "Old Chap" next'); or maybe the hall roof is leaking so please may the Guides meet in the church? The electoral roll wakes up . . .

Laying aside every weight . . . let us run with perseverance, said the writer to the Hebrews. He said a good deal more in this twelfth chapter, which is good study material for our subject. Indeed, until we proposed building operations, we probably had no idea that our church possessed so great a cloud of witnesses. We must therefore lift our drooping hands, strengthen our weak knees and not put out of joint those who are lame. We must strive for peace with all men; and all women; and much more.

It seems then, that we have embarked upon a public relations exercise. But let us forthwith resolve not to descend to unworthy PR tactics. Hebrews 12 will strengthen our resolve to steer clear of strife and to submit to God who is judge and to Jesus who is mediator so that at the end of the project we may offer to God acceptable worship, with reverence and awe.

Change is an inevitability of life. Everyone experiences it; everyone accepts it—except in church life. Change for change's sake (novelty; some new thing) is only to accelerate the roundabout which repeats itself and never gets anywhere. Change must derive from need. It is therefore fundamental that the Need for Change be specifically defined. A vague unease is not enough. Negative evidence (boredom; leaky roofs) will scarcely constitute a dynamic Need. Positive motivation (teaching; evangelism) will fire a congregation's imagination. Over a period, therefore. it will be necessary to prepare the minds of the constituents and to invite them to consider deep issues such as

> *What (or who) is the Church?*
> *What is its (or our) role in the world? Light, salt, leaven . . .*
> *How is worship best expressed verbally, posturally, musically,*
>   *mentally?*
> *How may the Word be communicated in public?*
> *Is sacrament essential? What do I mean by 'making my*
>   *Communion'?*

It will also be necessary to mount planned and persistent prayer. Outside help through illustrated lectures by specialists (including an architect) or a filmstrip such as those produced by Church Society on this subject will augment the programme. This booklet and its companion might even be considered helpful!

When the Need for Change has begun to win some acceptance, the PCC may be encouraged to appoint a small Working Party to look into parochial life and its buildings. The composition of such a Party should be carefully balanced and not left to spontaneous nominations, lest some vital part of church life is not represented. A total of six thoughtful members may be regarded as adequate.

In the interests of good PR the Working Party may deem it desirable to prepare a Questionnaire (see Appendix) which any member of the congregation may complete. Indeed, all who hold office *should* complete the form, and so should as many other people as possible. The form may then be returned to an appointed scribe on the Working Party or to an outside person working in strict confidence. The advantage of this lies in the chance to formulate more personal questions. Answering such questions is very therapeutic to some members of the congregation. They may even agree to sign the form.

The completed questionnaires require processing to provide a report. This distillation is what the Church is saying about itself. If nothing else happens, this will be worthwhile; people have been made to think.

The Working Party studies the report and patiently works through a procedure similar to that outlined in **8** and **9** above. It accounts to the PCC, who refer back their comments. The Working Party revises the proposals if necessary and, it is hoped, in due course the PCC will adopt these.

Consultations with ecclesiastical and statutory authorities will proceed and arrangements made for a special whole-church meeting which will enable the elected PCC to inform its constituents of its intentions and invite their support. Throughout this exercise, reporting must be thorough and well-mounted; the financial provisions must be spelt out. It may be assumed that if the proposals are courteously and painstakingly presented, support will be forthcoming from the majority of the membership. Brochures, leaflets or other accompanying publications must be convincing and typographically elegant.

The archdeacon (and, possibly, the rural dean) should be consulted early on and thereafter kept informed or even involved. They can be a tower of strength.

These consultative processes can be curtailed or they can be expanded into a full-scale social survey of the parish, with the whole congregation participating, although qualified guidance is essential, especially if interviewing techniques are involved. Other agencies such as the local authority or voluntary bodies may even be drawn in; dialogue can give way to multilogue. But we have outlined an average course.

11 PROFESSIONAL ADVICE

It is unlikely that the foregoing exercise can be accomplished without the participation of an architect, but not all architects can be experienced in ecclesiastical work, nor understand the manifold procedures in parish and diocese. Every PCC appoints its own architect under the Inspection of Churches Measure 1955 and it is hoped that this architect will be professionally and spiritually competent to advise on improvements to the accommodation. Perhaps 'spiritually' is too vague a term; obviously, the architect ought to be in sympathy with the ethos of the Church, he should be a fellow-disciple of its Founder, he should be aware of some of the niceties of churchmanship, he should be able to balance tradition and research. Professionally, apart from a knowledge of historical architecture and building construction, of statutory procedures and cost control, he needs to *care.*

It is strongly recommended that the architect be consulted as soon as the PCC appoints the Working Party. An architect is more than a draughtsman; he is trained to develop an enquiring and analytical mind which means that his contribution throughout ought to be vital. The worst situation occurs when a PCC calls in an architect and presents him with a schedule of accommodation.

The wise course is to commision a Feasibility Study to ascertain the options, taking into account the pastoral as well as the architectural factors. Only after further research on these options by the Working Party will a Brief be formulated to enable the architect to put pencil to drawing paper. The Brief will be a full statement of the required use of the premises.

The first scheme ought to be substantially the right scheme, subject only to minor adjustments, but in recent years the effect of inflation during the inevitable delay over formalities and during fund-raising has played havoc with carefully-planned schemes. Indeed, inflation has often outstripped the rate of subscription.

Advice on the appointment of an architect may be obtained from the Secretary of the Diocesan Advisory Committee or from the Secretary of the Ecclesiastical Architects' and Surveyors' Association (address from the Council for Places of Worship, 83 London Wall, London EC2).

An architect is bound by the Conditions of Engagement published by the Royal Institute of British Architects which sets out the scale of fees; the method of charging can therefore be agreed beforehand.

Special drawings will be required for presentation to the PCC and to the congregation. Small-scale plans are useless for this, especially as many people are unable to read technical drawings. Poster plans, set out simply, are necessary and may be of considerable size if everyone is to see properly.

If the scheme is of some magnitude, the approximate estimate may have to be prepared by a quantity surveyor; his fee is regulated by the scales of the Royal Institution of Chartered Surveyors and is also determinable beforehand. In certain cases site exploration may be necessary, involving a consulting engineer.

It frequently happens that a PCC will ask to visit projects carried out by an architect before appointing his firm. It should be noted that every scheme is tailor-made; no two situations or budgets are identical and therefore no architectural brief is repeated. Such visits can thus be misleading. Shopping around is no way to produce a purpose-planned solution to the local need. In seeking to establish references for an architect, it is more important to discover if he makes himself available when reasonably required, is inventive, informed, budget-conscious and everything else suggested in a foregoing paragraph. Ideally he should become part of the life of the church, though this certainly does not mean he should live in the parish!

Eventually, discussion must give way to decision. The responsibility for this rests firmly with the PCC but there will come a time when the architect as co-ordinator, as artist, as constructor, will have to apply his talents in a decisive manner.

12 NEW CENTRES

We have tried to demonstrate that new churches (or, rather, Parish Centres, leaving the term 'church' for the living occupants) need to be planned for 7-days-a-week use with maximum flexibility. Sheer financial considerations preclude the building of sanctuaries for liturgical use only. If it be objected that God is above economics and that there ought to be an exclusive building, a holy place, set apart for worshipping him, we are obliged to ask: what is worship? It can, of course, be moment-by-moment individual devotion but in our context it is what happens when two or three (hundred) are gathered together in Jesus' name.

And what does happen? The answer to that question will vary from church to church, from service to service, from week to week. The people present ought to be able to apply themselves, to become involved mentally and emotionally in the totality of praise, the corporate confession, the declarations and the proclamation. They ought to experience a unity with one another in their common fellowship with their Lord. We must never lose sight of these aspirations when designing new premises. The numinous quality of Christian worship in the Church of England must not be squandered. Undoubtedly the environment can stimulate worship, transforming the occasion from a mere meeting to a transport of homage.

This is not the place to discuss the difference (if any) between sacred and secular. There is a vexing dichotomy inherent in the subject and Professor J. G. Davies has written of this in *The Secular Use of Church Buildings.* It does, however, seem reasonable to set aside a place in a new multi-purpose parish centre where prayer may be made at any time without disturbance. This has the practical advantage that essential furniture for Sunday services may be left permanently arranged, thereby limiting damage due to handling and also reducing scene-shifting on Saturday nights. This, of course, assumes that the set-apart place becomes incorporated into the congregational space on Sundays, usually by drawing back folding screens.

An advanced example of sacred/secular 7-day integration occurs at St. Michael's, Paris, where the Anglican church centre is within a multi-storey office development in the heart of the city. It is a complex of auditoria and gathering spaces, with catering facilities, consulting and residential accommodation, all highly serviced.

The concept of a Parish Centre can best be illustrated by an outline plan. Obviously, in the absence of a *bona fide* site and a brief, this can only be diagrammatic.

The permanent chapel A could seat, say, 40. It is always directly accessible from the outside by the door B. For services where more than 40 are present, screen C can be opened to accommodate, say, 150 more in space D. This can again be augmented by opening screens into E and F as well as putting infants and parents into the soundproof rumpus room (or bawlroom) G, with relayed sound. Finally, if more space is needed for a large service up to 400 people, lounge L can be opened up. This lounge would be carpetted, with easy chairs and tables to form a fellowship area for after-service receptions. Here would be the bookstall. The lounge constitutes an intermediate area between street and sanctuary. The kitchen K, with outside access as well, could serve into E and L, possibly with two separate teams. Vestries and a council room are at J across the top. Cloaks are M and W.

During the week, the building would retain its chapel A and could accommodate a playgroup, smaller or larger meetings, making full use of folding screens which can now incorporate a fair degree of sound insulation. Remember, G is soundproof, so it could be equipped for stereo record playing; conversely, noise elsewhere would not disturb a committee or study group in here. Space F could be raised to provide a platform/stage and dressing rooms could be devised in adjacent spaces. Attractive access from the street presents no problems and such a building is capable of immense flexibility 7 days a week. Further facilities could include a caretaker's flat and a rugged games hall.

These facilities can also be incorporated in a church day school. We are not, however, required to duplicate the social services, though it is interesting to note how often local authorities will hire such premises for community purposes, ranging from art classes to senior citizens' welfare.

Such a scheme described above would cost a great deal of money and few such comprehensive projects have been built. A notable early project was St. Philip and St. James, Hodge Hill,

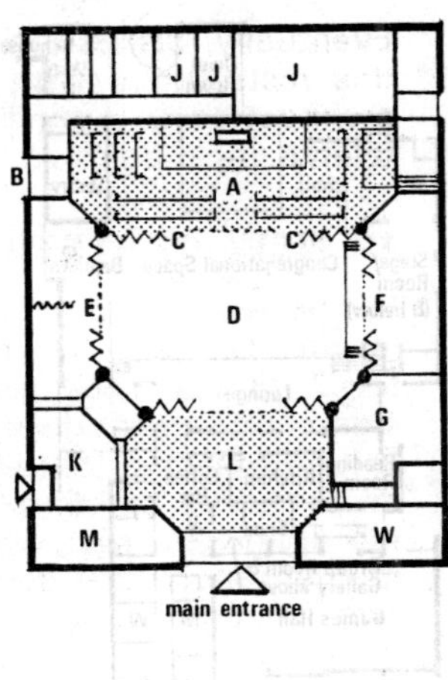

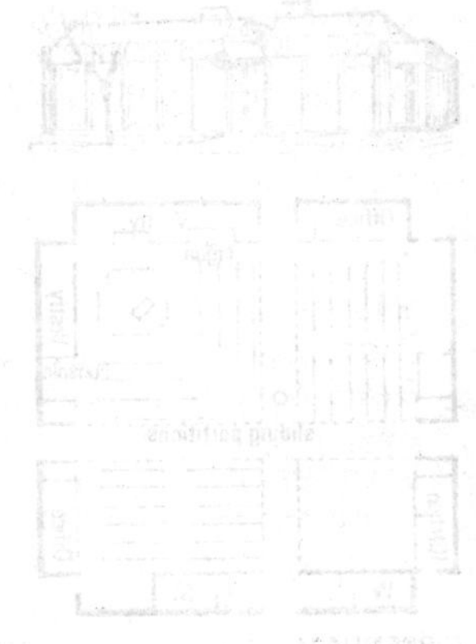

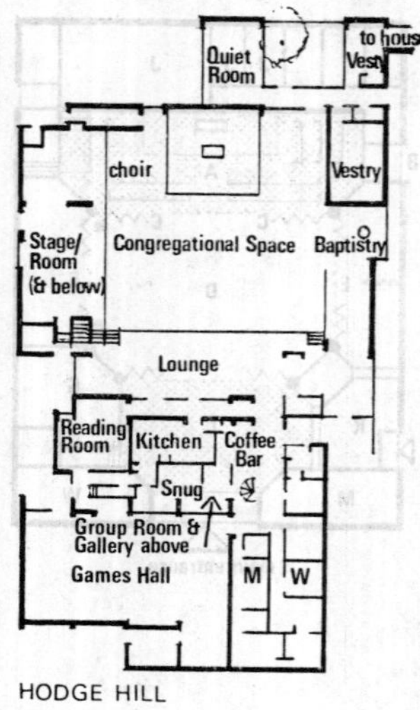

HODGE HILL

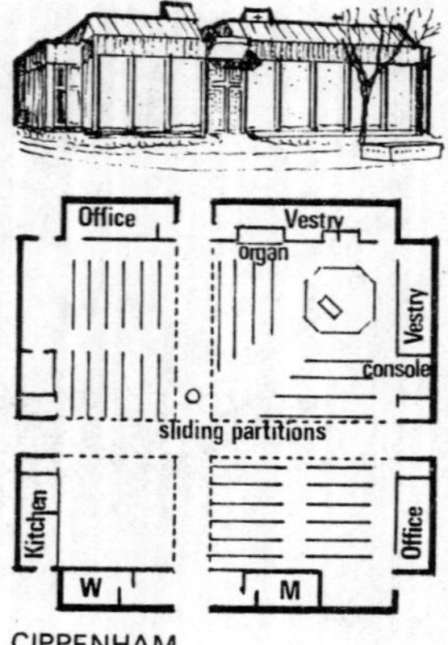

CIPPENHAM

Birmingham. This included most of the accommodation outlined above with the addition of a games hall and specialist facilities. There was, however, one fundamental difference: whereas the scheme above provides a permanent chapel with holy table and other minimum liturgical furniture (including organ) capable of being separated from the other main spaces, at Hodge Hill the sanctuary dais is permanently exposed in the main congregational space; in other words, there is no screen C as on our scheme. This was deliberate and was meant to unify all activity within a Christian context. It is a matter of opinion whether this has worked. Mr. Nigel Melhuish has written that, for most people, during activity other than congregational worship, 'the items of furniture in the sanctuary will only announce that "this space is reserved for activities which are not now taking place here". In other words, their message is negative . . .'

On the other hand, at the insistence of the local church, an oratory (or quiet room, set up with liturgical furniture) was provided and seems to have been appreciated, although it cuts across the intended comprehensiveness of the congregational space.

Much the same comprehensiveness applies at St. Andrew's, Cippenham, Slough, a superb piece of modern church architecture. This little complex is shared by Anglicans and Roman Catholics and was planned to have four main spaces, capable of separation by folding screens.

It will be noted that fixed pews are inappropriate in these multi-function buildings. Even if there is permanent seating (including choir) in a separate chapel A, pews engender a fence-like appearance and diminish the sense of corporateness.

There are two nettles to be grasped when considering multi-function of church premises. If a building is used for Sunday worship, ought it to be used for other activities? We have touched on this earlier, but the above illustrations highlight the point. Surely the rule is that if an activity is right in the sight of God, it is right anywhere, in one building as much as another. The limiting factor is whether any activity causes damage or unwarrantable maintenance costs. This leads to the second nettle: can space used for youth work also double up for adult meetings? The limit here seems to be whether ball games are desired; these require provisions such as wire guards, which are unacceptable to adults and destroy the congenial atmosphere. This is where a church day school can help. Hodge Hill incorporated a youth centre.

System buildings (sometimes called 'prefabricated') employ a higher proportion of factory-assembled units but still require foundations, drainage and other services, heating and decorating. The design must conform to the manufactuer's module. Sound insulation, maintenance costs and the actual size of foundations require scrutiny as well as a check on the extent and quality of the multitude of fittings required in a building. No package deal should ever be accepted without a quantity surveyor's opinion.

An experimental demountable ('relocatable') church was erected in Chichester diocese but it grew roots, pastorally as well as by virtue of the drains, electricity, water, foundations and pavings.

13 OLD THINGS MADE NEW

We may not be concerned with new projects but they help to illustrate points which also apply to old premises. And the Church of England has plenty of these!

We have already rehearsed the procedure for (mentally, at least) stripping a church of its contents and then indulging in the fancy of reordering and re-equipping .There are many completed examples of this process, in degrees varying.

A common desire is to shorten the nave by dividing it vertically half way along ,using the space behind the wall or screen for a gathering area or areas. The suggestion of an upper floor in this separated area is often canvassed. Depending upon the size of the church, all kinds of ancillary spaces can be provided, funds permitting.

St. John's church, Ealing, London, is a huge Victorian pile, rebuilt after a fire in the 1920s; it used to seat 900. The structure was strong and warranted major improvements (this is one of the first questions to be answered). Although the church was occasionally filled, the loss of 300 seats in pews was not regarded as disastrous, especially as the completed scheme allows an overflow of 200. A complex was formed across the

EALING St John's

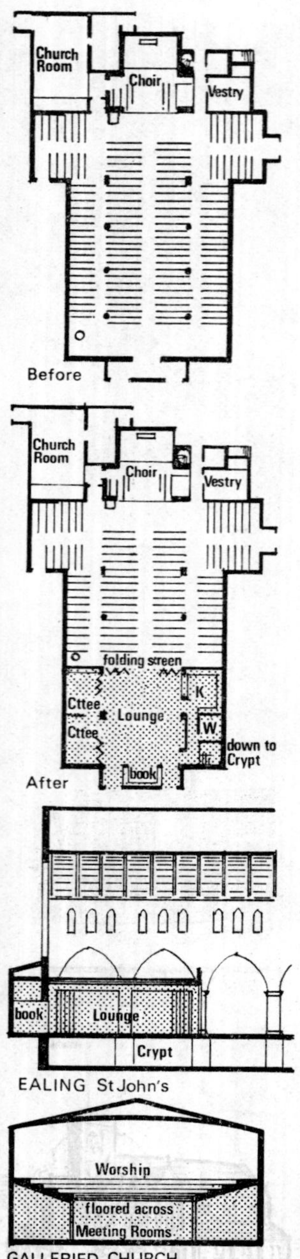

back half of the nave, providing a lounge, a pair of committee rooms, a kitchen, lavatories and bookshop. The large folding screens allow the lounge to be opened into the rest of the church to form the overflow mentioned above. If this had not been necessary, the screen could have been a fixed partition with pass doors. The lounge is fully carpetted and is furnished with easy chairs and other pleasant equipment. There is a ceiling and good electric lighting. The space above the ceiling continues to open into the loftier reaches of the nave; the PCC would have liked a meeting room above but the cost of such provision is extremely high. Furthermore, staircases are bulky items and reduce usable floor area. It seems that an upper hall is only feasible when there is an existing gallery; even then the floor of this needs to be levelled and in a lofty church the resulting upper space can be unfortunately proportioned. The wall between this space and the remaining part of the nave becomes a structural problem and may cut off west light. In smaller buildings (usually non-Conformist) the space between galleries has been floored and the worship area located at the gallery level (leaving the gallery seating ramped) but a lift is well-nigh essential, especially for weddings and funerals. Much depends upon the individual building and, despite the cost, substantial upper floors have been formed in churches where it was desired to introduce additional usage.

At St. John's, Ealing, the congregation can enter the church through the lounge and leave by the same way, pausing for coffee and chat, a most agreeable prolongation. The bookshop is strategically sited. But there is more to this lounge than a few cups of coffee.

Do we churchgoers realize that people are becoming afraid to enter a church? It is all rather out of date, a little spooky and holy, with queer language. They fear being conned into some religious lark which will make them appear faintly ridiculous and isolate them from their neighbours. Weekday use of the St. John's lounge is planned to offer a halfway house for strangers who would hesitate to plunge into a normal church, except as a tourist. In such a lounge they gain confidence; they come to realize that church members are not always nutty bigots and mealy-mouthed hypocrites. In due course a Guest Service provides the opportunity to welcome such no-longer-strangers into the principal activity of the rest of the building. This is two-stage evangelism and it should be remembered that responding to a coffee evening, or even a 'sacred' concert, may not be the same as responding to the challenge of the Word of God. It has also been found at Ealing that the lounge can be let to the local authority for a wide range of activities, as we suggested earlier. Not only does this provides welcome income but it is a means of introducing more people to the campus.

Following the success of this complex at church floor level, the PCC of St. John's promoted an even bigger complex beneath the church. There was an extensive crypt under the whole church but headroom was insufficient; accordingly the ground was excavated and there is now a series of games rooms, coffee bar, music rooms, workshops, group rooms. A playgroup meets in the mornings; the local authority also hires spaces and the whole place buzzes with young people in the evenings. No wonder the electoral roll is rising! An ecclesiastical fort has been converted into a Christian department store.

Such facilities must not be seen as a comfortable life-style for the congregation but as a base for a declared policy of outreach.

Not all churches are suitable for such development; St. John's, Ealing, is a mini-cathedral which had spare capacity. Not so Greyfriars church, Reading. They desired similar lounge facilities in order to develop their work in the centre of the town. Because there was no spare room inside the church, an extension was required. This was sited at the west end and, to follow the profile of the site, the extension was basically semi-circular. The church formerly ended at the great W window and the annex is a frankly modern piece of architecture, intended to harmonize with the old fabric. There is a semi-circular lounge divisible by folding screens into four compartments, a kitchen, servery-foyer, cloaks. Again, the decor is carpet, easy chairs, curtains and an atmosphere much appreciated by city centre businessmen who attend the weekly lunch (to mention only one evangelistic activity). Easy to enter, Greyfriars is widening its outreach.

READING   Greyfriars

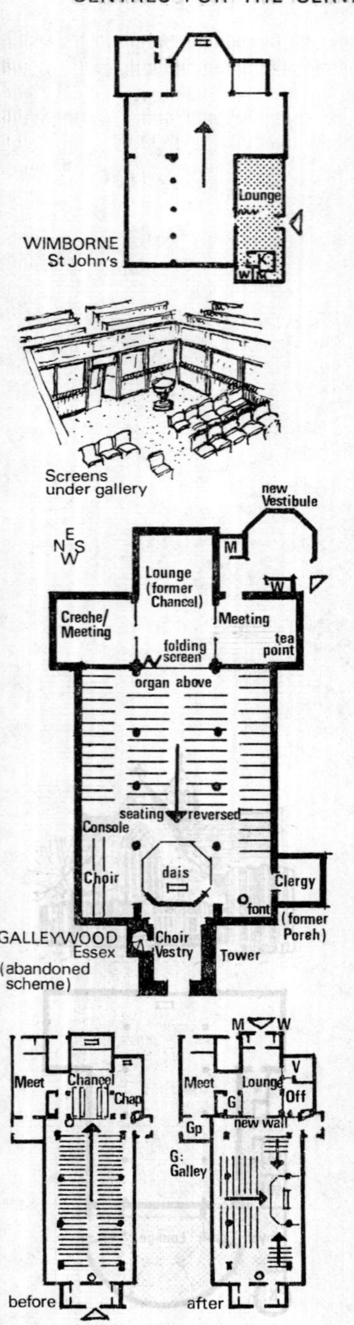

Not always will extensions be so dramatic as Greyfriars; or on the W end. St. John's church, Wimborne, Dorset, added a lounge-foyer on the S side, through which folk pass going in and out of church. A single folding screen allows one end to be used as a meeting room and there are catering and lavatory facilities.

Churches with galleries often present problems. Rarely does the congregation spread upstairs and if they occupy seats under the galleries there can be a lot of space between individual worshippers. Enclosing the space beneath the galleries by glazed or solid screens provides a useful meeting area as well as bringing the fellowship closer together. Nor is the cost abnormal.

There are many ways of reordering existing churches. The dais for the regular working area can be sited at the W end, releasing the chancel as a fellowship area. Or the dais can be on a side wall; visibility *through* an arcade can be better than looking obliquely *along* it. Or the working area can be central. In-built adaptability is the key; permanence is not always a virtue.

Up and down the country, dozens of churches have been remodelled. We have tried to illustrate typical examples but before we leave the subject we must summarize the operation in its historical context. In the companion booklet SHRINES FOR THE SAINTS: *How Parish Churches evolved,* we dwelt at length on the transformation of our church buildings by the Victorians. This was because much of our 20c ecclesiastical environment was determined between 1840 and 1880. We also touched on this legacy earlier in this booklet.

A small village church in Essex summarizes how an old fabric can be adapted down the centuries to successive contemporary requirements. St. Mary's church, Great Bentley, is basically Norman with a nave, chancel and W tower. Set in a generous churchyard, it has immense charm.

There may have been a church on the site before the Conquest but the present structure grew out of 12c beginnings. In the 13c some windows were changed and the font appeared. In the 14c the chancel was extended and the W tower arose. The N porch appeared a century later, followed by a pair of larger windows in the nave. Mr. Ian

Doolittle, in his notes on this church, records bequests for obits (memorial services on the anniversary of a death) and although the building was not large enough to contain chantries, the intention was the same. Other gifts went towards candles to burn 'before the image of Our Lady of Pity . . .' and towards the rood loft and a 'cope of red damask'.

At the Reformation there was the usual sale of trinkets ('2 cruets, one broken, a little crucifix . . .'), tabernacles, images; the altar was replaced by a portable table, windows repaired and walls whitewashed. The rood probably went at this time (1552) leaving the stone stairs on the N side remaining today. Two 'lecterns' were bought (probably reading desks) and a copy of Erasmus' paraphrase of the Gospels.

Haphazard seating would develop at the end of the 16c and in 1620 the inventory included 'the silver cup with the cover, a pewter pot, a surplice, a blue carpet (tablecloth) of silk and a white cloth for the communion table, the communion books and three prayer books and Jewel's "Apology" in English.' Apparently, Mr. Dernell held the 'great bible and book of Common prayer and the Register book . . . and the cushion and the hour glass in the church'. Mr. Doolittle goes on to record that 'in 1638 the churchwardens paid 4s 10d for a gallon of wine and two loaves for communion'. No insipid wafers! In 1606: 'the chancel wants pavements in divers places.'

In the 17c there was a gradual deterioration in the condition of the structure, with failing plaster and decoration. This was typical of the period and reflected the low ebb of church life in the village. By the end of the 18c the church had a Georgian appearance internally, with a complete system of pews continuous through nave and chancel on one floor level and incorporating a bay for the font (a focus at the W end), reading desk and pulpit (central) and the holy table (focus at the E end, though low profile). The whole arrangement, including the large gallery, provided a typical layout for Prayer Book worship. The stove adjoined the reading pew and the largest family pew!

In 1874 plans and specification were prepared for 'correcting' the church in the accepted ecclesiological fashion. The changes can be seen in the

GREAT BENTLEY

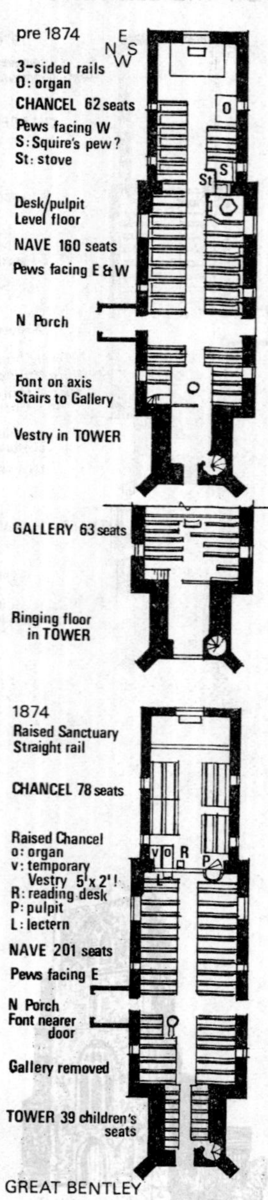

'before and after' pair of plans. They were typical of the period and were, briefly:

Removal of all pews; these were box pews with doors (except under the gallery, no doubt for peasantry). Along with the pew system went the 2-decker pulpit.

Removal of gallery.

New floors, about which there was much dispute with the builder, incorporating steps up to the raised chancel and again up to the sanctuary.

Replacement of 3-sided Communion rail (?Jacobean) by a straight rail.

New straight bench pews, those in the chancel facing inwards; they could hardly have been intended entirely for a choir since there were 78 places. There was no vestry and only a tiny temporary robing space for clergy behind the organ, which was removed across the chancel. In 1897 it was replaced by a new one. A vestry extension was obviously intended later.

A new semi-circular stone pulpit was proposed (at a cost of £15) but lack of funds reduced this to pine. A lectern was introduced, and a reading desk up in the chancel. The font was moved nearer the N door, off centre.

Children were relegated to 39 special seats as far back as possible under the tower. The total seating grew from 285 to 318.

Bellringers, having lost their staircase access to the ringing chamber due to the removal of the gallery, now had to climb a ladder and emerge through a trap door.

Old plaster was stripped and the walls replastered. Who knows whether whitewashed medieval frescoes vanished? The plastered ceiling of the nave barrel roof was removed early this century and the timbers are now exposed.

Those readers who followed the high-powered campaign of the 19c ecclesiologists in our companion booklet SHRINES FOR THE SAINTS will detect the influence of the Cambridge Camden Society at Great Bentley.

At the time of writing, a century after the Victorian re-ordering, new proposals are in hand for updating the old fabric which has seen so many developments. The chancel seating has already been removed and the holy table brought into the centre of the chancel. It is now the turn of the nave; a modest gallery has already appeared in recent years, with access from the ringing chamber (via the ladder!). The organ is already in the gallery, which is good siting.

Further work will see the gallery completed, and fitted with a spiral staircase. Ringers will then abandon their ladder because a lavatory and a tea-point will be formed in the tower at ground level. By removing some pews, a meeting area will be formed in the W half of the nave. Curtain and track will enable this area to be screened from the rest of the nave, access to which is only through the reception area. It is here that refreshments will be served after services or during recitals and concerts when the whole church is in use. By drawing the curtains closed, the reception area becomes suitable for meetings. (A similar use of curtains has been operating at Cudham church, Kent, for some years but there the reception area is in a side aisle).

At Great Bentley, floors will be carpetted, heating and lighting modified and a determined effort made to centre the village life on this gem of a building. This is true conservation, more than mere preservation. An ancient building is being given yet another new lease of life without tampering with the structure which has seen so much life and death these last 900 years.

14 EQUIPMENT

In the past, church halls have commonly been provided with a kitchen large enough to serve the Ritz, although the appliances are hardly of the same standard. While it is appreciated that many such kitchens have served as social centres for lady helpers, the economic facts of life now prohibit this. Even if there are harvest suppers every month it is possible to operate in a relatively small space provided it is properly designed. In most church kitchens, for example, everything happens at or below worktop level; wall space above is squandered. Storage is unrelated to usage, resulting in excessive handling with consequent breakage and reduction of hygiene. Surfaces are unsuitable and equipment is obsolete and wasteful.

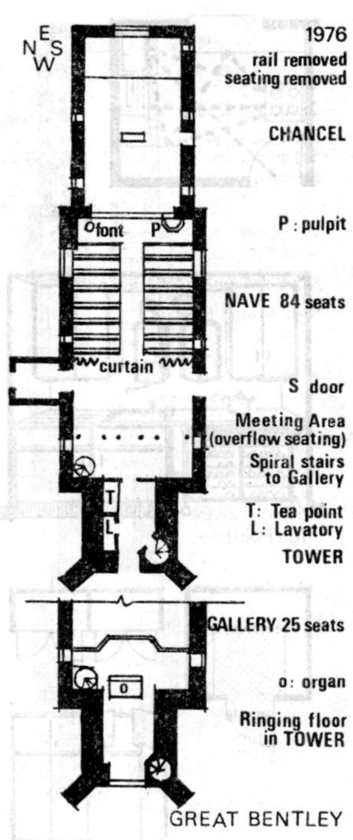

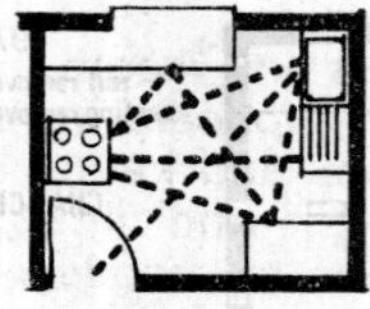

Tea Point

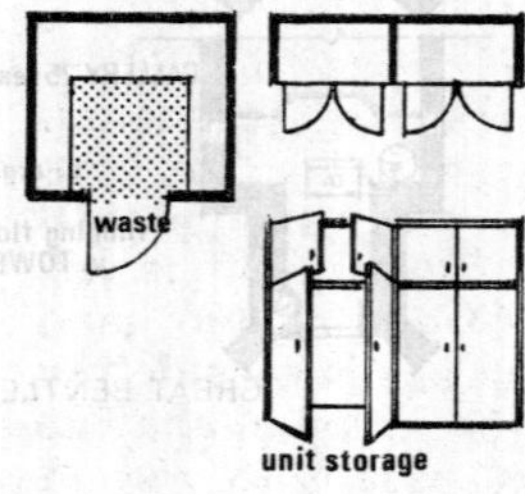

unit storage

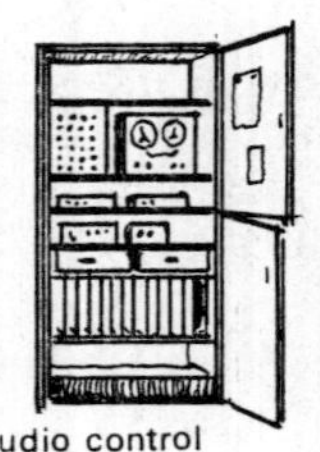

Audio control

Just as we carried out our earlier investigation on the usage of church premises, so we may examine the function of a hall kitchen. It may help if we regard it as a galley and prepare an inventory of essential equipment. A diagram of our existing layout, with work-journeys plotted on it, will reveal the need for a designed work flow.

We have mentioned tea-points, which are usually required in the church to serve a reception or fellowship area. These can be formed in a space hardly larger than a domestic wardrobe. They need a worktop, a sink and drainer, water boiler, storage units and a trolley which can be used as a mobile servery. Ventilation is needed as well as a lockable screen or shutter across the front. The cleaner's store may adjoin.

Storage is a subject requiring specialized treatment. Store *rooms* become junk rooms. A basic principle for designed storage is to schedule the items essential to each organization, then provide cupboards as generously as possible. Each organization should have its own cupboard(s), usually in two heights from floor to ceiling if this is practicable. These cupboards can be in ranges and less than 1 metre deep; in other words, not walk-in. Standing space is not storage space. The organization should hold a key to its storage and woe betide any equipment not put away!

There has been an impressive expansion in church bookstalls in recent years, with consequent gain in cash and education. Modes of display are important and smart layout pays dividends. It is possible to form an effective sales display on bracketted units obtainable from the do-it-yourself shop. Good lighting is essential and there ought to be a substantial till or a steel wall moneybox. The display will need regular re-arrangement, with special lines publicized from time to time; some churches do well with greetings cards and stationery. Rotating bookstands can be obtained from library fitters but too large a selection can be self-defeating.

Audio-visual equipment is regularly found on church premises. Of this there is a bewildering range. The one universal concomitant is Wire! All the components in an audio system must be linked by wire. How much better, then, if a building can be wired for sound, with audio sockets as frequent as power sockets. Into such wall sockets can be plugged the jacks and DIN plugs associated with amplifiers, microphones, tape recorders and record decks. The cables (some screened) are wired back to a control cupboard in which the above gadgetry is assembled (and kept under lock and key). Closed circuit TV has been incorporated in some places. Slide and film projectors need storage and there is a case for securing them to mobile projection stands. Fixed projection screens are not always desirable if a flexible seating pattern is desired. Audio-visuals are here to stay and they form a technical subject on which specialist advice is recommended.

Car parking on site, if required, will be considered in the planning application but may need to be related to the entrances to the building.

Nothing tarnishes a building more than ill-placed notices, outside or in. Or outdated notices. Or badly printed. On internal walls, pinboards or magnetic boards are essential; no-one should be allowed to use drawing pins or adhesive tape on normal surfaces. In a new building a comprehensive system of well-designed and co-ordinated signs enhances the place.

And it must surely go without saying that cleanliness is next to godliness!

Church premises (including halls) are places of public assembly. There is therefore the same element of risk that attends any large gathering anywhere. Apart from structural stability, the major hazard is fire. Too little attention is paid to this, as any architect who undertakes quinquennial inspections will confirm. No doubt the Ecclesiastical Insurance Office will echo this assertion. This is more than the provision of one or two hand appliances. The full treatment of this aspect of church use is outside our scope but any alterations to church property ought to be vetted by the Fire Prevention Officer, who will also advise on means of escape as well as detection and extinguishment of fire. The insurance company should also be notified when building work is in hand on churches.

15 FINANCE

This is not a booklet on stewardship or fund-raising but the cost of even a modest improvement scheme is likely to take some people's breath away. It will certainly be said that the church at home should not feather its nest in the face of the needs of overseas churches. A commendable sentiment.

It is, however, arguable that the church in Britain is in a missionary situation and that in the past, compared with other types of buildings, churches have received inadequate maintenance and modernisation. We have left it dangerously late, for if there is a declining church in Britain, what price the mission field?

But this is to beg the question. Can it be established that investing parish funds in new buildings, or improved buildings, manifestly enables the work to expand? The evidence so far is that the processes outlined in this booklet do stimulate the congregation to consider

their raison d'etre
their responsibilities
their outreach
their giving

but it must be based on prayer and teaching. It will not happen automatically.

Obviously, finance is intrinsic to any building or furnishing scheme and the implications must be faced; moreover, they must be faced with a sense of proportion, neither looming too large nor being played down. It is possible for the financial aspects of a proposal to take over and become the dominant issue; any PCC member knows this only too well. On the other hand there is a naive other-worldliness which says 'We believe this is of God; we will go ahead and trust him to provide. We will go ahead in faith.' To which must be asked 'Whose faith?' The answer is all too frequently: the builder's, or the architect's! They are the ones who are being called upon to exercise faith—that they will be paid!

At the outset, a responsible fund-raising plan should be prepared, broken down into units which ordinary members of the congregation can appreciate. One hundred people giving £1 extra per week for three years will produce over £15,000. And we all know about tax covenants.

16 NO NEED TO FEAR

'In the land of the blind, the one-eyed man is King' said an Oxfordshire vicar. We live in a land of spiritual blindness and many of us are one-eyed Christians. We have nevertheless a kingly task of leadership in opening people's eyes and turning them from darkness to light.

Our buildings are tools in our hands. Our craft of disciple-making needs fine tools. The Church goes out and it comes back in; when it comes in it needs accommodation and equipment. It needs an envelope, a built environment, in which to gather, where the Word may be taught and visually demonstrated through the sacraments of the Gospel.

Our buildings are a means to an end. If the means are a hindrance, how may we accomplish the end? To be a working Christian is a mighty serious occupation. We have seen that it is a full-time occupation which needs every device and assistance human ingenuity and fellowship can provide. When we have given all, then (and only then) dare we look up to God to make it work.

The pair on the Emmaus road heard the Word from its Source. Yet they failed to recognise him until he demonstrated a characteristic action in a building. Then their eyes were opened . . .

APPENDIX   Draft Questionnaire

1.1   Reason for questionnaire (how it will assist development of church life); state of existing church activities and buildings.

1.2   To obtain the widest views, the PCC invites all who are active in the work of the church to complete this questionnaire and post it by . . . in the attached addressed envelope (may be addressed to the architect).

1.3   Your response is CONFIDENTIAL and will not be returned into the parish. Replies will form the basis of a balanced report to the PCC. In due course you will have an opportunity of discussing the report and any proposals which may emerge.

2.1   What is your special activity or responsibility in this church?

2.2   Are there developments in church life which you would like to add to present activities? Could these take place in existing premises? (here follows a list to spark off suggestions).

2.3   If you lead or assist in a group or organization (or would be willing to lead a group arising from 2.2 above) please state:

Name of group (or type, if not yet started)	heating is/not adequate
	lighting/power is/not adequate
Number of members	any other difficulties?
Average attendance	Have you ever met elsewhere?
Age group(s)	Is this convenient?
Day(s), time(s) of meeting(s)	Do you require outdoor space?
Could you meet at any other time?	Is your equipment adequate?
If so, when?	If not, please enlarge
Where do you meet?	What change in numbers do you expect in the next five years?
This meeting place is	Which of these activities apply to your group:
too big/right for size/too small	
uncomfortable/adequately furnished	lectures/discussions
suitable/unsuitable for present work	films/slides
except for . . .	study groups/prayer meetings
in particular for . . .	bookstall/display
toilets/cloaks are/not adequate	singing/musical
storage is/not adequate	ball/table games
catering facilities	tea/coffee
are/not adequate	parties/squashes
are/not required	buffet/sit down meals
not/easy for members to get to	any other?
not/easy for parking cars/cycles/prams	Would you meet jointly with other groups?
	If so, which?

Please delete or amend as necessary.

2.4   If you are engaged in an activity outside an organization, please state what it is. What facilities do you need?

2.5   What do you specially value about life in this church? Is there anything you would wish to change? Is there anything you would wish to retain at all costs?

2.6   Any other comments?

2.7   THANK YOU . . . Please sign here...date...............

This is only a draft. There is no direct mention of church services. Allow space for answers.

This questionnaire is an aid to consultation, not a substitute for it.

BIBLIOGRAPHY

The Secular Use of Buildings. J. G. Davies. SCM Press.

University of Birmingham: Institute for the Study of Worship and Religious Architecture. *Research Bulletins* and other publications, especially *Problem Churches.*

Tired Dragons. E. C. Lynn. Beacon Press, Boston, Mass.

Victorian Essex. Essex Record Office: Publication 40.

St. Mary the Virgin, Great Bentley. I. Doolittle.

Church Society filmstrips. *Where did you get that Church?* and *What can you do with that Church?*

St. Francis' church, Duston, Northampton. *Architect:* A. S. B. New FRIBA.

St. Andrew's church, Cippenham, Slough. *Architect:* W. S. Hattrell and Partners.

St. Philip and St. James, Hodge Hill, Birmingham. Live Projects Department, Birmingham School of Architecture (Director: Professor Denys Hinton) in conjunction with the Institute for the Study of Worship and Religious Architecture, University of Birmingham. *Project Architect:* Martin Purdy.